GIRL

POWER

THE CRIMSON KISS QUOTE COLLECTION

II

CICI.B

Dedicated to my Crimson Kiss Squad,
always.

After all, these quote collection books
were created because of y'all.

GIRL POWER

Ahh, life.

Life, as a girl.

Life, transitioning into womanhood.
Life, as a woman.

It ain't always easy, is it?

We've got to deal with men and their shit. Heartbreaks. Periods. Period cramps. Mood swings because of periods and cramps. Entire human beings growing inside of us. Thousands of different ads, commercials, and billboards telling us who and what we should like. Social media. Instagram "body goals." Instagram "couple goals". Pressure to have a "fat ass and a flat tummy". Pressure to style our hair in a manner that is "acceptable" for work. Pressure to cook five-star meals, even if cooking isn't something we all are good at, because that's part of being a "real woman". Pressure to be book smart, but not too book smart (because then we think we're know-it-alls). Also, be sexy, but not too sexy (because then we're hoes). Pressure to use our voices, but not speak too loudly, or too much (because then we're annoying and need to be silenced by a man).

Pressure to settle down, "get wifed" and have kids by a certain age. Pressure to live our lives, carefree, but only up until a certain age. Pressure to wear thongs, even if we hate feeling like there's dental floss between our ass cracks, because God forbid if someone sees our panty line through the fabric of our dresses, skirts, pants and shorts. Make sure we wear bras, because it's not appropriate to be without one in public, but if we're out in public and our bra strap shows... holy fuck...

Sound the alarm.

Decide not to breastfeed your child, and you're an absolute monster. Breastfeed your child in public, and it's indecent exposure. Go figure.

Oh, and let's not forget there's the government, forever trying to pass new laws that will strip us of the choices we make with our own bodies.

If that's not already enough, and I've barely scratched the surface, we have society constantly pitting women against each other.

It's fucked.

Sometimes, being a girl, being a woman, fucking sucks.

But, being a girl, being a woman, is also fucking dope. And maybe we don't give ourselves enough credit sometimes. Maybe we don't give other women around us enough credit. Yea, we go through a lot. But damn it, we also get through a lot.

We are strong.

We fight for what we want, and what we believe in.

Resilient.

We may fall, but we know how to get right the fuck back up.

Brave.

We stand face to face with a lot of bullshit and don't back down for shit.

Determined.

When we really want something, nothing and no one can stand in our way.

Supportive.

We'll go to the end of the earth with the people we love, just so they don't have to go alone.

Nurturing.

That shit is second nature to us, many times, even first.

Self-sufficient.

We know how to figure out a way to get the job done for ourselves. If there's no door for us to open, we fucking make a damn door.

Opinionated.

Yea, they try to silence us.
But um … *fuck them.*

Compassionate.

We give a lot of fucks actually, about many things.

Confident.

Chin up. Back straight.
Ask permission from who? For what? To slay the day? To slay our lives?

Mmmm, I think not.

Vulnerable.

We lay it all out there. We let people in. We cry. We scream. We explain our feelings. We expose ourselves. I don't care what anyone says… there's so much beauty in that.

We are **Inspirational. Powerful. Unapologetic. Charismatic. Diverse. Intelligent. Ambitious. Encouraging. Motivational.**

We're so many amazing, different things at any given time. Sometimes, we're everything all at once.

But all of it is a choice, though. A choice that is, and always will be ours to make.

GIRL POWER

GIRL

POWER

Some people, while cloaked in an invisible blanket of disaster, alone, decide to question the Universe and everything in it, then throw blame at the Universe and everything in it. Then you have others, in the same blanket, in the same solitude, who decide to peer inward and question themselves.

"Why am I here?" "How did I contribute to being here?" "What parts of me are hindering me more than they're helping me?" "Who am I right now?" "Who do I want to be?" "Has the way I've been living my life thus far been beneficial to my mind, soul and heart?"

See, throwing blame at everything and everyone else is easy. Peering inward however, now that's a challenge. Often, we'll see things within ourselves that we don't want to see. Parts of ourselves that are toxic, not only to us, but to others too.

And that hurts.

I was someone who decided to peer inward. Of course, seeing what I saw about myself, made me want to run in the opposite direction, deny those parts were mine. I wanted to leave them where they were and pretend they weren't there. But I didn't do that. I knew that if I wanted a better life, I had to become a better me; which meant taking accountability for myself.

Was it hard? *Absolutely*. Was it a lot of work? *Fucking, yes*. And it still is. Working on yourself isn't a "one time only" thing. It's a lifetime thing. But isn't everything worth having in life hard, and a lot of work? So there I was, cloaked in an invisible blanket of disaster, alone, face to face with the ugliest parts of me.

And I decided that the woman I wanted to be, for myself, was the thing worth having in my life.

Going through it...

We're Only Fucking Human.

"I don't care how strong I am, how independent I know I can be, how capable I am of picking up my broken pieces and keeping it moving—I get tired too," I confessed to my girl Erika. "I have a good heart and I know that's a good thing, I do. I'm also very aware that everything in life happens for a reason. I get it. But honestly, sometimes I just get tired of being the good girl with the good heart that people are so fucking reckless with. I get tired of being 'the practice chick'—the girl that dudes learn a valuable lesson from and then go off and be this great fucking guy for someone-fucking-else. I mean, don't get me wrong, I'm happy they're able to learn from the bad shit they did. I truly am. I'm just fed up of being the one they learn from. Do you understand what I'm trying to say?"

She nodded her head in agreement. "I do," she said. "I really fucking do." I sighed and shook my head, "I'm sorry. I'm just having one of those fucking days."

She put her hand up. "Nah, don't you dare be sorry for venting girl. We all have days like this. We're women. But before that, we're only fucking human. And this thing called life, definitely ain't always easy."

Flower Girl.

I remember being a teen, picking up flowers, plucking their petals one by one and reciting, "He loves me, he loves me not. He loves me, he loves me not ..." It was something all of my friends and I did back then, just for fun. But man, who would've thought that we'd all grow up, to have moments in our lives when we'd recite those same words, except now, we were dead ass serious about wanting and needing an answer.

<u>Woman Power.</u>

Someone once told me that part of women empowerment, was to tell the truth. There are some things that people say to me, that stick with me, forever …

That, was one of those things.

Super Facts.

"You drop everything for him, all the time. Tell me, what has he dropped for you again? Oh, that's right. Nothing. Wake up," she said, clapping her hands together. "He ain't the one!"

I winced a little as Erika and I sat listening to our girl Angel give our other girl Jazzy some real talks. Both Angel and I were the "tough love" types, and everyone knew it. However, there are levels to everything in life, and Angel was way tougher than I was. Her patience was way thinner than mine was too. If there was one thing that she hated, it was to see her girls stuck on stupid over men who continued to show that they weren't good ones. Being a no-nonsense type of woman, she often spoke to us the same way she spoke to herself—logically and harshly.

Did she come off a little too harsh at times?

Fucking, yes.

But did she usually end up saying some shit that we needed to hear?

Fucking, yes.

Jazzy sat with her head down, tears pouring down her face. She too knew that Angel was making sense, and that what she was saying was dead on. Nevertheless, it still hurt. I understood that. I reached under the table for her hand and squeezed it. My little way of saying, "You know how Angel is. She ain't trying to hurt your feelings on purpose. She just loves you, a fuck ton, and wants to see you get out of this shit. We all do."

She squeezed my hand back. Her way of saying, "I know, I love you guys too."

God bless silent friendship codes.

"You're letting him mind-fuck you." Angel continued. "Don't you see? Lemme guess, he told you that no one's gonna want you after him. That no one's gonna love you after him. That without him, you'll have nothing. Right? That's a MIND-FUCK from an insecure ass little *booooy*. See, all that shit he's saying to you, is just a reflection of how he feels about his damn self. HE's the one worried that no one else will want him, if YOU leave. HE's the one worried that no one else will ever love him the way you do. HE IS THE ONE who feels like, without YOU, he'll have nothing, and that no one will care because deep down he knows that he's the one who AIN'T FUCKING SHIT. He's just scared that one day, you're gonna wake up and realize it too. You're letting an insecure ass boy, mind-fuck the shit outta you. Don't say no one ever told you so."

The Power Within.

I don't want to be the girl who spends her life pretending to be happy. Pretending like the things that she yearns for deep down inside, aren't that important. The girl who spends her life waking up every day, dragging her feet, to get ready to go to a job that she doesn't love at all, but simply settles for it because it pays.

The girl who sleeps and wakes up beside a man who she wished would be more attentive to her soul—the part of her that matters the most.

The girl who loves romance, forehead kisses, and all of the other physical gestures of affection, but spends her life pretending like all of those things aren't that big of a deal to her because she's with a man who isn't into that kind of stuff or thinks it to be "corny".

I don't want to be the girl who pleads for a man to love her properly.

The girl who settles for people and things, all because she thinks it's better than having no one and nothing.

I don't want to be her, and yet, I look into my mirror and there she is—staring at me through dull, tired eyes.

The girl I don't want to be, is the girl I am now. I can either stare at her and feel sorry, or I can take full control and change that girl's life.

Right now.

Calling It Like It Is.

"Funny how you want a good woman," I said to him, "But have no desire to be a good man to her in return."

Closure 101.

"Crazy how I'm back here again. No?" I said to Jazzy. She looked at me, "Back here? Where?"

"Back with this whole, 'seeking closure' shit. Like man ... you would think that heartbreaks get easier over time because, well, been there, done that— right? But they fucking don't. You still end up having those moments when you just torment yourself by going over every little detail in your mind of where/how things went wrong. Ugh ..." I plopped down on the sofa beside her and put my head back. "I'm exhausted. My brain hurts."

"Want some wine?" She asked. I turned my head toward her and frowned. "Is that even a real question?"

She smiled, left the room, and came back with a bottle of Pinot Noir and two glasses. She filled them both and handed me one. "Thanks boo," I told her. "I gotchu," she answered. We sat lost in our own thoughts for a bit, and then she broke the silence.

"You know, B … you did everything that you could do," she started. "You tried everything that you could try. You did what you were supposed to—stayed loyal and stuck by him even in the worst of times. You gave him your best, your all, and maybe that right there should be your closure. Maybe that should be enough for you to realize that you're probably better off without a person who doesn't appreciate or respect your love."

Cradling my glass, I nodded my head, "You right," I said staring at the wall. Then I turned to her, "*Shiiit*, actually, you so right that you should probably be using your own advice for yourself and your situation." Jazzy nodded her head. "You right," she said. "Well, ain't we just a couple of right ass muhfuckas, sippin' red wine in the middle of the fucking afternoon," I stated, and we both laughed.

"Ahhh man," Jazzy sighed. "Love you, B."

"Love you back, Jazz."

Taking A Stand.

"You must stand up for what you believe in," they kept saying. So one day, I did.

I took a deep breath, straightened my back, then stood up tall and confidently for myself.

Amour.

After all of the shit I've been through when it comes to relationships, and all of the many times I've been hurt, let down, betrayed and disappointed, people always ask me if I still believe in love.

I guess it's a normal question.

And I guess if I said that I didn't, people would more than understand.

But I still believe in love.

Of course I do.

I *love* love.

Love is magical. Love is powerful. Love is healing.

Real love, is absolutely beautiful.

It doesn't matter how many times my heart has been broken, there's nothing that could ever make me say "fuck love"
...

I *am* love.

New Me, Fuck You.

Back when I didn't know who I was, I cared a lot about what other people thought of me.

But now that I know who I am, other people's thoughts about me don't fucking matter.

Queen of Hearts.

I wear my heart on my sleeve.
Always have, always will.
And actually, I'm finally
okay with that.

Devil Penis Magic.

Amongst other things, I feel like part of coming into my womanhood was when "good dick" no longer clouded my judgment or made up for the lack of other things of major importance that should always be brought to the table.

Things like:

Would he be a good father if he got me pregnant?

Can his ass hold a job?

Does he have his own shit?

Does he pay his immediate bills, and put some cash aside for a rainy day, or is he spending his cash on stuntin' for the gram'?

Does his ass have fucking life goals?

Is his ambition UP?

Forget being my man—will he be able to be my partner and my best friend through all the highs and the lows?

I just feel like part of coming into womanhood was when I started to realize that these things really fucking mattered. Because a man who only has good dick to offer and nothing else, is bound to set me back and fuck up my entire life.

<u>Rebel Girl.</u>

I'm that girl.

The girl who doesn't respond well to commands. The girl who rebels against anyone who tries to control her. The girl who refuses to sit still inside of a box that society decided was best for her, with her mouth shut and hands tied behind her back. I'm the girl who will scrape, gnaw, crawl, and bleed her way out of such a box, then set it on fire and watch it burn. I'm the girl who will fight for what she believes in. The girl who will loudly remind others that she is an individual in this world, and won't apologize for exercising her right to be that.

I am that girl.

So the quicker you get it through your head that I am not yours or anyone else's property, the easier you'll find it to get along with me.

<u>Actions.</u>

His problem?

He thought he was the only one with other options out there.

So I had to show him that, you know, he wasn't.

Getting through it ...

GIRL POWER

Time Out.

"It's like now that I'm finally trying, you're not paying attention," he said to me. "Oh, no no, I see you trying," I answered calmly. "It's just that, well, I'm finally over you. Your efforts came about six months and a couple of days too late."

Debt Collector.

I stopped focusing on what he was or wasn't doing, and started focusing on what I was or wasn't doing—for myself. Get it?

It was never his responsibility to make me happy. It was my responsibility to make myself happy. He didn't have to love me the way I deserved to be loved. I'm the one who had to love my damn self the way that I deserved to be loved.

No man owes me anything.

I owe myself ... *everything.*

<u>Choices.</u>

"... And another thing!" I yelled, turning on my heels to face him. "Quit telling people that you 'lost me', as if you're some sort of victim in this whole story. Try telling the truth for once in your miserable life—YOU HAD SOMETHING GOOD, AND YOU FUCKED IT UP ALL BY YOURSELF. How many more chances did you expect to get, huh? How many more tears did you think I was going to give you? 'Lost me', HA! You didn't lose shit. You had two choices—to do better, or to stay the same. Ironically, I had the same two choices as you, but you chose to stay the same, I chose to do better and fucking leave."

Grounded.

Maybe after years of going through/putting myself through the same shit with different men, I've finally learned my lesson. Maybe for the first time, my heart and mind are both sitting on the same page.

Maybe, for the first time in my life, my feet are planted so firmly in my wants and the things that I know I deserve, and are taking up so much space, that the excuses I once held onto and used to defend the fact that I was constantly settling for everything less, literally have no room to breathe—let alone to grow.

Maybe it's a combination of it all. Who knows? But whatever it is, it immediately turns me all the way off from any man who starts to smell like bullshit.

It immediately blocks any thoughts of "give him one more chance" from making it anywhere near my soul.

It forces me to never again think of apologizing to any fucking man for wanting better for myself.

Whatever it is, no matter where it came
from, I'm just glad it's here.
God knows, I know, my friends know ...

it was about fucking time.

I've already had my fair share of
handsome devils. I'm ready for a
handsome gentleman now.

<u>I know what I know.</u>

I'm not interested in a man who feels like he needs to "handle" or "put up" with me. I'm interested in the man who feels like loving me exactly the way I am is the best fucking thing that ever happened to him.

I don't want a man who's going to scream, call me names, or belittle me should I happen to make a mistake or do something that may not sit right with him. I want a man who will sit me down and communicate with me, respectfully.

I'm not trying to be with a man who will be bothered by my success, due to his own crippling insecurities. I'm trying to be with a man who will never miss an opportunity to tell me that he's hella proud of me, clapping the loudest while he cheers me on.

At this point in my life, without a doubt, not only do I know that I deserve someone who will be for me what I am for them, but I also know that I am not fucking asking for too much at all.

The Importance of Self-Awareness.

This is what no one ever says, but should:

Sometimes, the negative energy that you blame everyone else for, is really coming from you. Sometimes you're your own storm. Your own toxin. Your own monster.

Sometimes you're the one making a mess of your own life. Your relationships with other people are constantly strained because your relationship with yourself is constantly strained. You're the one who isn't growing while everyone else around you is. You're the one who doesn't know how to deal with the frustrations of your own life, so you take it out on others.

Sometimes, it's hard to believe that other people around you have already fought their own demons and won, because you're still fighting yours.

You're not always going to be the best version of yourself in every moment of your life, but if you're never willing to be open to the idea that maybe it's you

with the problem, and not the ones
you're so busy blaming ... then how can
you ever be at your best?

<u>Toxic Fantasy.</u>

You wanna know what it was?

Somewhere in the middle of our relationship, when his true colors started to show and hurt, I fell out of love with him. I started creating this sort of fantasy/idea in my mind of who I hoped he would eventually become for me, and fell in love with that. Needless to say, I learned the hard way that people don't become who you want them to, if that's not who they were meant to be.

Truth Hurts.

No one really likes to admit it, but the truth is, often we break our own hearts by staying in situations that we know aren't good for us.

<u>On to the Next Store.</u>

"Maybe we've just gotta start doing the same things with men that we do with the shoes we try on in the stores," I told Jazzy. "Put them on, walk around in them a little, and if they just aren't fitting right, leave them right there and continue shopping for the perfect fit. On to the next store—you know? We can't force shoes to fit; they either do or they don't. And we sure as hell don't buy them if they don't fit us right. So why do we cling to this bad habit of getting with men who we know damn well don't really fit us right, staying with them, and trying to force them to fit anyway? I'm just sayin'... think about it."

Merry-Go-Round.

One of the healthiest things I have ever done for my life was holding myself accountable for the roles that I played in my own heartbreak. You know—fool me once, shame on you, but fool me twice then that shit's on me. It was so easy to sit around with my girls and be coddled and listen to all of the things I wanted to hear, "He's a piece of shit." "You deserve better." "It's not your fault."

And maybe all of those things were true the first time around. But what about the second time? And the third? And the fourth?

How could I deserve better if I kept going back to the same piece of shit? How could it not be my fault when he'd already shown me who he was? I chose to keep believing his words over his actions. How could I not be the one doing anything wrong, when I kept ending up at the same fucking dead-end, heartbroken, with a face drenched in recycled fucking tears?

Come on. Seriously.

Blaming the same man for doing the same shit over and over again wasn't getting me anywhere. My choices had me sitting in the exact pile of shit I deserved to sit in. The only way to get out of it was to start by holding myself accountable for my own damaging behaviour.

Mean What You Say.

"Thing is," I said to Jazzy, "when we say that we want better for ourselves, we've gotta really mean that shit. When we say that we deserve better from a man, we've gotta really mean that shit too. Otherwise, we'll keep sitting in the same bullshit, sounding like a played-out song on the radio that everyone is fed up of listening to. We've gotta erase the phrase 'easier said than done' from our vocabularies. I swear to God, all that phrase does is set us back. It keeps us lazy and miserable. That fucking phrase is just one big excuse not to face ourselves and do the work we so desperately need to do from within.

We all go through shit—all of us. And most of us get it wrong a lot of the time. No, it's not always easy to figure out how to get shit right, but isn't it worth a try?

We sit around, spend years praying and fighting for one man to love us the right way. What if we took those same prayers and use that same fight towards learning how to love OURSELVES the right way? I'm just sayin'..." I stirred the ice in my drink with the straw, "At some point man, we've gotta get fucking real with ourselves out here."

Save The Drama for Your Momma.

With "bad boys" comes fucking drama. I've stopped inviting drama into my life.

No, I don't want a "bad boy who's only good for me". Thank you, but I'm grown now and that bad boy shit isn't cute. I want a good man, who's a good man.

Period.

Good men are inspiring. Good men are lit. Good men have their priorities in check. Good men are LIFE. If I'm going to be about any kind of man, I'm a be about a GOOD one.

Bullshit-Free Zone.

Yes, he's going to have to step it up to get to me because I for sure won't be stepping down to accommodate any man ever again. I'm already not the type to entertain just anyone, so should he happen to get my attention, then yes—he'll have to work to keep it. And don't get it twisted here, this isn't me saying that I have a "one-way street" attitude, and won't lift a finger to do my part—nah. I'm definitely the type of woman who loves to cater to her man. I won't challenge his natural instincts as a leader, but I'm also smart enough now to know that there are two types of men out here:

One who will lead his woman the right way because he's good within himself. And one who will lead his woman the wrong way, because he isn't good within himself.

So the moment I feel like a man is about to lead me somewhere destructive and toxic—I'm out. I will vanish from his life forever.

I'm not sticking around for the bullshit.

Actions vs Words.

We teach people how to treat us—we all know this.

If we want to be respected, then we have to respect ourselves first.

See, we have no problem screaming to men that actions speak louder than words. But why can't we also scream that to ourselves? Because every single time we stick around, or continue to go back to someone who treats us like shit, or makes us feel like shit most of the time, what we're showing them is that it's okay. We're letting them know that we accept being treated like shit. So in the end, we're fucking ourselves over ...

Our actions as women speaker louder than words too.

Fucking, over it...

GIRL POWER

Access, Denied.

Keep your filthy fucking hands
away from my clean heart.

Take No Shit.

And oh, how they *looove* a woman who
won't take any shit from anyone, until
they realize she won't take any shit
from them either.

Low Key Preparations.

I think it all started when I stopped liking him. I still loved him, but I didn't like him anymore.

That's when I knew my mind was preparing my heart for that moment— the one where I'd say, "I'm done" and really mean it.

Know Yourself.

I fucking hate it when guys like you call women like us, "complicated". It disturbs parts of my soul that I didn't even know existed because we're NOT. All we want, is for the person we're with to go as hard for us as we go for them.

Balance. What's so complicated about that? Nothing.

What's so wrong with that?
Fucking, *nothing.*

But see, guys like you will make it seem like it's the most unnatural and worst thing in this world—and for what?

Oh, because you got lazy. Because you got selfish. Because somewhere along the line you decided that you didn't want to do your part anymore, but wanted us to continue doing ours— think about that.

Are we really complicated?

Or are guys like you making things complicated with your bullshit, one-way street mentalities? Know yourself.

Super Simple Shit.

"I just don't get it," I said to him. "If you don't know how to be in a relationship with someone at this point in your life, either let someone teach you, or stay single. If you don't know how to treat a woman at this fucking point in your life, either LET someone teach you, or stay the fuck away from us."

<u>Boy, Bye.</u>

Neglect a woman for long enough and make her feel like the basic shit that she asks for—which she shouldn't even have to ask for to begin with, is "too much."

Eventually, she's going to leave you.

House of Cards.

I can't believe this is happening
with you of all people.

You were supposed to be different.
Life with you was supposed to be
peaceful.

But here we are—fighting.
Arguing over the same shit you said
you'd never do.

I should have known all those promises
you made when we met
were just too fucking good to be true.

Shooting Stars.

The guilt always catches up to guys like you when you least expect it.

And then you start wishing that you treated girls like me just a little bit better than you did.

You Ain't Ready for A Woman Like Me.

"I warned him," I said. "Told him that I had learned so many lessons from my past mistakes and I had grown. See, when you're pursuing a woman who's out here making shit happen for herself you can't be half-assed, and you can't come with reckless behaviour. Because a woman who's out here making shit happen for herself is only interested in a man who's gonna be an asset in her life—not a fucking liability. I warned him," I continued, shaking my head. "But like a child, he just didn't listen. And I stopped babysitting children a long ass time ago."

<u>You Reap What You Sow.</u>

"That girl's heart didn't deserve to be dragged the way it was dragged by you. Sit tight, sir. You gon' learn today."

Love,

Karma.

Dope Ass Woman
With A Dope Ass Heart.

It was around 8pm when I emerged from the shower.

It had been a long, stressful day and I was glad it was over. After drying off, I piled my messy curls on top of my head, secured them with a clip and threw on a pair of sweatpants with a hoodie I had made that read "Dope ass woman with a dope ass heart". I stared at myself in the mirror, and smiled. "Damn straight you are. And don't you ever fucking forget it."

After fixing myself a plate of red grapes and assorted cheeses, I poured a nice full glass of Pinot Noir then headed to my living room and plopped down on the sofa. "Fucking, yes," I said out loud. My plan for the rest of the evening was to relax, and watch one of my favorite movies *The Devil Wears Prada.* Just as I made myself comfortable and took my first sip of the rich wine—the phone started ringing. "Oh for fuck's sake!" I exclaimed, highly annoyed. "Why didn't I turn this shit off?" I put down my glass and reached for the phone. "*Maaaann,*"

I rolled my eyes at the sight of the name glowing on the screen.

Don't answer it. Part of me said.

No, just answer it because if you don't, you know he's only gonna call back. The other part of me said.

"Gawt damn it!" I shouted, and hit the answer button.

"Hello?" I said into the phone trying not to sound as annoyed as I was.

"Hey," he responded, and I rolled my eyes again.

"What's up?" I asked.

"Nothing much, just chilling. You?"

Is he really calling me just to like, shoot the shit or something? He can't be serious.

"Same." I said dryly.

"Oh okay. So how are you?"

Oh my God.

"Bro, can you cut the shit please? Is there something I can assist you with? Is there something specific you would like to say or get off of your chest? 'Cause to be quite fucking honest, I'm not in the mood to play pretend with you. K? Let's just skip to the real reason why you called. What's UP?"

"Oh, so I'm bro, now?" He asked, insulted.

Hang up the fucking phone in his ear, my inner voice said.

"Well you definitely ain't fucking BAE anymore!"

"Look, I didn't call to argue," He said, switching gears. "I called because … well, I'm sorry."

I was getting more annoyed by the minute. "Yes, I know. You've said that a thousand times. You've left it on my voicemail. You've texted it. You said it to all of my friends and then asked them to pass the message along. You've written it on every card to go along with the dozens of roses you send to my house every other week. I KNOW!" I felt my blood starting to boil. Normally at this point, tears wouldn't be far behind, but I didn't feel like crying. Weird, right?

I don't know what it was, but I had no tears left for this bullshit.

"B, if you could just let me explain." "Absolutely not," I said calmly into the phone. "God. I've heard your piece of shit explanation already, and I've heard hers too. And they mean fuck all to me. Fuck. All. You know what? I take back what I said at the beginning of this conversation. I don't care if you have something to get off of your chest—go get a diary and fucking write it down there, because I truly am NOT interested in hearing it. Nor am I interested in giving you anymore of time. You fucked up. You know you fucked up, and you're sorry—I get it. Trust me, I get it. But you being sorry won't change what you did. It won't change the way I look at you now or the way I feel about you now. Everyone has their limits--their boundaries. Lines that once you cross, you can't cross back over. I had a line ..." I paused for a second and sighed. "And you crossed it. And now you've gotta stay on the other side of it, away from me."

I didn't even give him a chance to respond. I hit end, blocked his number, then silenced my ringer all together. "Enough," I said.

I put the phone down, put a piece of cheese into my mouth and thought for a second as I chewed. "Fuck him. And fuck her. Matter of fact, they might as well keep fucking each other."

Then I grabbed my glass of wine, took a large sip, and just like that went back to my originally scheduled evening.

New Beginnings.

That liberating moment
when you finally realize
you don't need him
or his shit at all.

To Love Yourself, Is to Protect Yourself.

Sometimes you've just gotta say no.

No. You may not come back into my space. No. You may not take any more of my energy. No. You may not call or text me. No. You are not welcome to exist in my life any longer, boo.

No.

Save Yourself the Heartache.

Can't fuck with people who don't
actually give a fuck about your feelings.

That's how you end up breaking your
own heart.

This Woman Right Here.

I'm still gentle, caring and nurturing.
But I'm also no longer afraid to be
assertive.

I'm still as ambitious as I ever was.
But I no longer let men who aren't on
my level, try to make me feel like I need
to slow down so that they can catch up.

I'm still willing to fight for love.
But not for a man whose idea of that
is a woman sticking around while he
betrays, disrespects, embarrasses and
hurts her repeatedly.

I'm still willing to compromise.
But not at the expense of my mental,
emotional and spiritual health.

I'm still the woman who will give my
one hundred percent.
But not for a man who will only give
fifty percent in return.

I'm still the women who loves.
I'm just no longer a sucker for love.

Sea of Delusions.

He'd broken every woman
he'd ever met.

And yet,

he still didn't think he had a problem.

Ashes to Ashes.

Today someone asked me what I was leaving behind as I move forward into the New Year.

Out loud I responded, "Anything that hurts me more than it heals me." But in my mind to myself …

I thought of your name.

Survivor.

This is the part of my life where I silently remove anyone who hurts me more than they love me, drains me more than they replenish me, brings me more stress than they do peace, and tries to stunt my growth rather than encourage it.

I've done more than enough talking and trying to make things work with certain people.

I'm done.

<u>Game Over.</u>

It's been a couple of months since I disappeared. My number has changed, so has my address.

I have to admit, I'm a little surprised that you're still looking for me. Still asking people to relay your messages filled with apologies and desperation. And if I didn't know you any better, I might be impressed. Touched by your determination. Tempted to hear you out one more time.

If I didn't know you any better, I might feel like this time around you finally understand and want to be good to me. But here's the thing …

I do know you better.

So stop looking for me. Stop asking for me. I'm not going back to you, ever.

<u>Red Light.</u>

You can't force someone to love you the way you love them, or even to love you at all.

And you shouldn't want to anyway.

<u>The One That Got Away.</u>

"He knows," she said. "Every time he sees you out and about, smiling and enjoying life, or hears about all of your amazing accomplishments he feels that little pinch inside of him. He knows that you're the one who got away, and he's got no one to blame but himself."

<u>For Me.</u>

He's got to love me.

And not just because of the way that I make him feel about himself, but also for all of the little things that make me, well, me. Things about myself that I would try to change or even bury once upon a time because some other man made me feel bad about them. You know?

Like the way I'll start dancing in the middle of a store if a song that I love comes on, not thinking or caring about who's watching. The way that I laugh at my own dumb ass jokes all the time, even when no one else gets them. The way that I get loud when I get excited about something. The way that I'm determined in life, period. The way that I love romance. The fact that I'm sensitive as fuck. I'm the girl who will cry when the dog in the movie we're watching dies. He can't be the guy who rolls his eyes and tells me to 'stop being so extra', but rather be the guy who smiles, wraps his arms around me and says, 'it's okay'.

Like I said before, these are little things, but they're important little things. They make me who I am; and it took me a long time to love who I am so he can't love the person he wants to turn me into.

He has to cherish and love—me.

Gratitude.

I'm not the same girl I used to be and I'm not sorry about that. It's called growth—and I thank God for it every day.

Loyalty on Reserve.

"You're different," my home girl said with a warm smile as we walked toward my car.

Living in two different cities, it had been a while since we'd seen each other. She was in town for the weekend, so we went for dinner and drinks to catch up. "I know I am," I replied, proudly. "Well, whatever it is you started smoking, be a good friend and puff puff *paaaass*," she said as we both fell out laughing.

"You're an ass," I told her. "But nah, truth be told, I've just had a series of back to back realizations in my life. You know? Like just a bunch of shit that has hit me hard and I guess, woke me up. I've been hella unfair to myself throughout the years because my mindset was backwards as fuck. 'Thugging' shit out and staying 'loyal' to situations and people that were no good for me, thinking that was how you proved your love. That was how you proved you were worth it." I laughed as I heard myself say that sentence out loud—staying loyal to situations and people who were no good for, or to me.

God, the old me truly did have a backward ass mindset.

"Pure bullshit," I continued. "The only fucking thing that I was proving, was that people could do or say whatever the fuck they wanted to me and there would be no consequences, ever. The only thing that I was proving, was that I was down for the disrespect. How gross of me? No, honestly. How fucking *grooossss* of me! I got tired of myself is what it was, girl. I got tired, and annoyed of my own shit so I flipped the script and decided, enough. You know how people love to say, 'Don't change for anyone. Be exactly who you are'?" She nodded her head.

"Okay, well that's bullshit, because sometimes you need to fucking change some shit about you, for you. I desperately needed to change some shit, so I did, and now my loyalty lies with those who respect me the way I respect them and those who know how to reciprocate the love I give them. My loyalty is RESERVED for the healthy shit in life, not the toxic shit. Period."

My girl snapped her fingers and then high-fived me. "Honey, *preeeaacch*!" She yelled. "You had me feeling those words deep in my damn soul! I feel you, one hundred percent, and I'm fucking proud of you." She pulled a cigarette out of her tiny Chanel clutch and lit it. After blowing the smoke out into the night sky, she pointed at me. "You need to write that shit down and put it one of your books," she said. I nodded my head and smiled as I reached into my clutch and pulled out a Super-Slim of my own. "I think I just might." I agreed. "I think I just might."

Self-Love.

Now that I've learned how to love myself the way I needed to love myself, there is no more room in my life for shitty relationships.

<u>Exit Stage Left.</u>

No ex-boyfriend, I don't want to hang out and catch up sometime with you. I don't want you to check up on me, nor do I want to receive, "Remember when we used to..." or "This made me think of you," texts. I don't want random, "Hey, I'm in your area, let's grab a bite to eat." or "What are you up to today?" calls. And I for damn sure don't want you to tell me that you often miss what we once had.

What I do want is for you to respect that I've moved the fuck on.

I may have forgiven you for the shit you've done in the past, but that is not an open invitation for you for you to be a part of my present.

You're an ex for a reason.

So whether I'm currently involved, or single as all fuck, there still isn't any room for you in my life. Get it?

I do not want to be your gawt damn, muthafuckin friend.

Russian Roulette.

"Do you regret it?" She asked me.

"Regret what? Being loyal to him?"

"Yeah," she said. "Do you ever wish you would have just said 'fuck it' and did your own thing regardless?" I thought about it for a second. "Not at all," I finally answered. "You wanna know why? At the end of the day, I can sleep well at night knowing that I did what I was supposed to do. Granted, I may have done it for the wrong man, but that's life sometimes. Right? You never really know what you can expect from other people. It's always a gamble. You can only put your best foot forward, do what's right and hope for the best in return."

The Art of Release.

Sometimes we have to let go of the men that we love, let them go out there, and figure out how to be men for themselves first.

Because a man who doesn't know how to be a man for himself can't ever be one for a woman.

Self-Respect.

To be honest, I'm just trying to treat myself better than I ever have.

That's all.

Self-Defence.

I can forgive you and genuinely mean it, but still never want to be around you ever again. I'm allowed to protect my peace.

Matter of fact, I'm supposed to.

<u>Set Yourself Free.</u>

If I didn't forgive him,
he would have owned me forever,
and he'd been my master for long
enough as it was.

My Reflection.

Broken men dressed as knights in shining armor used to flock to me. I couldn't seem to escape them. They were all I attracted. Polished, strong, and secure on the outside. Rusted, weak and insecure on the inside.

Why me?

Because like them, I too was broken. But unlike them, I knew that at some point I had to break the cycle of brokenness. At some point, I had to fix myself.

I mean, if not, how else would I ever attract anything else?

The glow up ...

A Teacher Named Heartbreak.

If you're open and willing, a heartbreak can teach you so many things about yourself. Things you didn't even know you needed to learn. It will show you who you were, who you are, and give you a good kick in the right direction toward the woman you want to become.

But only if you're open and willing.

Ambition 101.

In the past, I've gone extremely hard for the men I was with. Pushing and helping them to build their careers from the ground up and achieving all of their goals while putting all of mine on the back burner. Needless to say, when those relationships ended, those men went on with everything. Myself on the other hand, well, I didn't have much, physically.

But the one thing those experiences did leave me with, were lessons. Granted, it took me a couple of tries to grasp those lessons, but I eventually did.

Nowadays, I unapologetically put my own goals at the top of my list. I go hella hard for myself before I'll go for anyone else. And no, that isn't to say that I won't ever help or go hard for a man that I'm with again. It's just that I won't put any man above myself. Nor will I choose a man who would ever want me to do such a thing either.

Queen Behaviour.

This morning I woke up and reminded
myself that my soul is fucking beautiful,
my mind is fucking powerful, my heart
is made of fucking gold, and that I've
got so many gawt damn good things
going for me, that I literally do not need
anyone who isn't going to love me the
way that I fucking deserve to be loved.

Backbone.

I stopped doing everything that everyone else wanted me to do.

I stopped listening to what everyone else thought would be best for me and my life.

I stopped waiting for other people to get their shit together.

I stopped fighting with other people to be for me what I was for them.

I cut off men who weren't acting right.

I cut off friends who weren't acting right.

I stopped entertaining bullshit.

I stopped giving people my best while they were giving me their worst.

And as a result,

I glowed the fuck up.

The Journey.

Some days, I have to remind myself that things are always going to work out the way they're supposed to, no matter what, and that wherever I am in my life at the moment, is exactly where I'm supposed to be.

<u>My Own Best Friend.</u>

I talk to myself a lot.
I know that sounds crazy. But is it?

I live with my body, no one else.
I live with my mind, no one else.

I live with my heart, soul, energy and intuitions, no one else.

I know myself better than anyone else.

So is it really that crazy for me to discuss important life decisions with myself before turning to anyone else?

I think not.

Before I can be anyone's best friend and voice of reason, being my own first is imperative.

Self-Reminder.

You wouldn't be besties with someone who uses you, takes advantage of you, makes you feel like you aren't good enough, puts you down, neglects you, treats you like absolute shit and makes you cry all of the time. Would you? No.

So why sleep with and stay with a man like that?

The only thing that separates a "friendship" from a "relationship" with a man is sex really. If it's not okay for your friends to treat you badly, then it should not be okay for any man who walks into your life either.

Moving Forward.

"Did it hurt to walk away?" She asked.

"Of course it hurt. You don't walk away from the person you love with joy rushing through your veins. You walk away feeling like you're being gutted on the inside with every step you take. But even though I was hurting pretty badly, I knew I had to take those steps away from him with faith. Faith that time, coupled with moving forward with my own life would eventually heal me. God knows that I had put enough faith into staying, and that shit wasn't working. It was time to put it into something else.

And that something else was me, walking away."

<u>Survivor.</u>

The scars on my heart will tell you the
stories of war;
but the way it glows and still beats so
strongly ...

will show you who won.

Advice to My Twenty Year Old Self.

I know you swear you're grown and everything because you pay bills and shit, but you absolutely are NOT.

So yes, you are too young. Too young for a gawt damn boyfriend. You need to ditch his ass and get to know yourself first.

Figure out who you want to be in this world for YOU, not what some boy who hasn't even figured his own shit out yet wants you to be for him. You wanna date every now and then? Cool. But date for FUN. This is not the time for you to be "building" with no dude. This is the time for you to be building with yourself.

Laugh more. Go on those road trips. Take more pictures with your home girls. Also, fucking chill on your shoe addiction. For the love of God, you don't need a new pair of shoes every week—I promise. Instead, use that money to BOOK FLIGHTS. Go! Get the hell outta here! See the world and have fun! There's nothing holding you back. You're twenty years old baby girl.

It's okay to be the young girl that you are. Stop trying to grow up so fast ...

trust me.

Who the Younger Me Needed.

The younger me always had a hard time standing up for herself, and because of that, people walked all over her—a lot.

The younger me was often afraid to speak up for herself, and because of that, she ended up staying in situations that either hurt her or made her extremely uncomfortable. The younger me was desperate for love from a man. Not having a father growing up, she craved that male role model in her life. And because of that, she was easy prey. She often fell victim to men who took advantage of that craving by being controlling. The younger me was highly insecure about the color of her skin and what was on it. Ninety percent of her body was covered in aggressive eczema, and her caramel complexion often drew the type of attention that she didn't want at all.

A few years ago, I vowed to be better to myself. I got up close and personal with all of my self-harming layers and decided to strip them down, one by one, and create new layers from scratch.

Today, I stand up for myself assertively.

I speak up for myself when I feel like something isn't right or when someone isn't treating me the way I deserve to be treated.

I've accepted that I'll never have a father. It is what is. Learning to love myself freed me of desperation. It allowed me to make better decisions when it came to men.

I know now that the color of my skin is beautiful.

I understand now whether my eczema is aggressive on some days or dormant on others that this is what God gave me, and whoever has a problem with it, that's exactly what it is—their problem.

Today, I can say with confidence and a full heart that I am the person the younger me needed.

Let's Get Fucking Real.

"The bottom line is this," I told her handing her a tissue so that she could wipe her tears. "And I'm not gonna sugar-coat the shit I'm about to say, so if you'd rather not hear it, then let me know right now and I'll keep my mouth shut." She inhaled deeply, straightened her back, and then exhaled. "No, I want to hear it. Shit, whatever it is, I probably need to hear it."

I sighed as I got flashbacks of the times when I was in her shoes and shuddered. They definitely weren't the proudest moments of my life. That was for damn sure.

"Listen," I continued. "It doesn't matter how many people tell you that you're worth more. It doesn't matter how many of us tell you that you can do so much better than the shit show of a guy you're settling for. We could gather the whole squad and have all of the fucking kumbaya moments in the world, and it wouldn't matter because you've gotta believe all that shit yourself. We can't walk away from your situation for you. And trust me, we'd all love to, but you've gotta be the one to decide that you need to. We all know and believe that this bullshit isn't for you. But you're only gonna walk away once *you* know and believe that it isn't for you.

Maybe right now you're not supposed to be in a relationship with anyone else but yourself. Maybe this is your time for you and you're supposed to be enjoying it for exactly what it is—your time, for you.

No distractions. No compromises. No thinking twice. No checking with someone else. Instead, a time to figure shit out for yourself. Start something new for yourself. Learn something new about yourself. Travel. Explore. Stay out late. Go to bed early. Build new parts of yourself that you always wanted. Big chop your hair and grow it all back healthy. Do your thing and fall in love with that."

Without warning she flung her arms around me and hugged me tightly. "I hate it when you're right." She whispered. I hugged her back just as tightly. "I hate it when I'm right too sometimes." I said as we shared a small laugh.

"Ugh, MAN!" She let go of me, stepped back a bit, and sighed. "I can do this, right?" She asked. "Girl," I started. "You can do anything you want to do for yourself the moment you decide you actually want to do it."

True Strength.

You know what true strength is?

It's being able to be honest about moments or times of weakness.

Admitting that you don't have your shit together the way you would like to.

That you're a little, or extremely lost. That you're in fact not the well put-together person you've been pretending to be.

That you don't have all of the answers. That you're battling with yourself. That you don't know what the fuck you're doing.

That you're scared.

That you're damaged.

That you're mean to people sometimes, simply because you're wholeheartedly unhappy with yourself. That you're currently not the best version of yourself, but you want to learn how to be.

That you need help.

That you're incredibly insecure and broken on the inside, and because of that, you lash out at people who don't deserve it.

True strength is being able to get a fucking grip of yourself, be humble for a change, and admit that you are not immune to the dark shit life throws at everyone from time to time, and that you're actually smack in the middle of it, but want to learn how rise above it.

Own your truths, and set yourself free.

Life after the glow up ...

<u>Golden.</u>

"Your heart is clean," She said. "You don't have trust issues because you yourself are a trustworthy person, so you tend to see everyone else in the same light. You look for the good in people before you think about the bad. You give people the benefit of the doubt before you ever consider them evil or malicious. The word jealousy isn't a part of your vocabulary because you aren't a jealous person. You root for people to win constantly. Watching others rise inspires you, even during the times you aren't doing too well in your own life. And that is why you can't imagine others being jealous of you, or even worse, silently wishing for you to fail."

I remember going home that night. I replayed what she had said over and over again in my mind.

Fuck man. She was spot on.

School of Hard Knocks.

We all know the saying, "If you want to know who your real friends are, see who's still around while you're down on your luck."

But, actually, I learned there was another side to that coin. A side I wasn't ready for at all.

I found out who my real friends were once I started making some amazing moves in my life by chasing my dreams. Once it was clear that I was on the verge of a come-up, I started noticing some salty ass behaviour from certain people around me, which slowly progressed into their outright hatred of me. That shit crushed my heart. It was probably worse than any heartbreak I had ever experienced with a man. These women were supposed to be my *friends*.

It's crazy how life works sometimes.

You can be broken as fuck on the inside for a long time, but then realize one day that isn't something you want to feel anymore. So you woman up, and do what you need to do for yourself.

You start fixing your broken pieces.

You stop complaining about all the things you don't have, and start genuinely appreciating the things you do have.

You start treating yourself better.

You start loving yourself better.

You start realizing your worth.

You get into your own lane, and mind your own business.

You start doing what you love to do.

You start working hard at what you love to do.

Your hard work starts paying off.

Your shit starts coming together.

You start feeling better.

You start sharing all that you've learned freely.

You're proud of yourself, as you should be.

You're genuinely happy, and now you completely understand the saying,

"Happiness comes from within" because all of this happiness you're filled with, you've created for yourself.

But then you look up, and realize there are people who you love and who have had front row seats to all that you have been through in your life in order to get to where you are now, who instead of being proud of you and happy *for you*, are actually upset at you for fixing yourself and your life. It's just crazy.

I guess it's true what they say though: *some people are okay with seeing you do better, as long as they don't feel like you're doing better than them.*

Growing Pangs.

The problem was, for a very long time, people in my life were used to me never saying much. They were used to my timid mannerisms and extreme dislike for conflict of any sort. It made me someone they knew they could get validation from. Someone who they could always depend on to agree with them, even if deep down, I didn't.

I was the perfect nutrient to nourish a person's superiority complex. To them, being around me not only meant that they were always in control, that they never had to worry about me saying the opposite of what they wanted to hear, and never "calling them out". But it also meant they always had someone to be "above".

Many years later, I grew out of my timid ways and into my voice—into confidence. I began speaking up for myself and *against* whatever I disagreed with. Conversations with some of these people thickened, and conflicts did arise. I wasn't afraid of much anymore. And they didn't like that shit.

The moment I began to slowly build a healthy relationship with myself, is the same moment all of the unhealthy people around me who used to, "love me for exactly who I was" began despising me.

Fucked up, I know.

But to be honest, looking back, I'm glad shit worked out the way it did. The Universe was simply showing me the people who didn't deserve to be around me as I prepared to rise to new and exciting levels in my life.

Don't Sleep on Yourself.

Life is too short to be stressing, worrying, crying, and questioning your worth because someone (relationship, friendship or otherwise) can't or doesn't want to treat you right. Seriously, take it from someone who's been there, done that, and freed herself from it all. There is life after heartbreak and separation.

And if you just give it a chance, you'll find out that it's actually fucking beautiful.

In My Own Lane.

I do my own thing.

You won't see me everywhere with everyone. You won't see me with just anyone. I'm selective with my circle and who I go around on purpose.

I'm not down with the gossip.
I'm not here for the bullshit.

My desires don't include wasting my time and worrying about everyone else's business when I've got my own to worry about. I have my own shit to get done.

I've got real goals that aren't going to reach themselves. I've got real dreams that aren't going to work unless I do. My life and my accomplishments are serious to me.

I know where I'm supposed to be now. And I stay far away from where I'm not supposed to be anymore or ever again.

And that's how I avoid unnecessary drama.

Plot Twist.

Some women are single as fuck, and are actually having the time of their lives. They're building careers. They're accomplishing goals. They're traveling the world. They're discovering things about themselves that they love while shedding old layers of themselves that they don't need. They're unlearning old, bad habits while practicing new, healthy ones. They're embracing their alone time and thriving in it. Contrary to the shit that the masses like to spew, not all single women are lonely, bitter, miserable or damaged. Some women are single as fuck, and are more in love with their lives than they ever have been before.

<u>More Self-Love.</u>

Whether I'm in a relationship or as single as it gets, I've learned that either way, I always need to make sure I matter to myself first.

End of story.

Self-Sufficient AF.

You have to trust yourself enough to go after what you want, and trust yourself enough to also let go of the shit you don't need in your life.

Want the career of your dreams?

Go get it.

Guy you're with is making you miserable?

Fucking, DUMP HIM.

Friends behaving more like enemies?

Throw their asses in the trash too.

And if you're reading this right now, thinking to yourself, "Easier said than done", perhaps you explore the fact that you've just made an excuse for yourself. Give your head a shake and tell yourself this instead, "It'll be hard, but I'm going to do it."

Give yourself pep talks.

Be your own cheerleader.
Be your own life coach.
Go to yourself for relationship advice.
Learn how to trust *yourself.*

G.T.F.O.H

"Do you think men are intimidated by you?" She asked. "I'd hope not," I responded through laughter.

"I mean, shit, why would they be? Because I'm not down to beg for things? Because I'm not down to sit around and wait for things to magically fall into my lap? Because when I want something, I work my ass off for it? Because even though I fall a lot, I always figure out a way to get right back up? Because I don't make excuses, instead, I make solutions? Because I ain't over here with the back of my hand on my forehead, in 'distressed-damsel' mode, aspiring to be 'saved' by some dude on a white horse?"

I laughed again. "That would be sad as fuck. The way I see it, the only men who would ever find me 'intimidating' are those who either don't have their own shit together and feel insecure about it, are flat out lazy/ambitionless, but still want to be respected and acknowledged as 'THE man,' or prefer women who have less than them, which is sad as fuck! I don't know about anyone else, but those types of men definitely aren't what I want in my life anyway."

Served.

"I'm not the type of woman who needs a man to validate my existence," I said to him nonchalantly. Immediately, his expression changed, and I watched as he quickly scrambled to mask it. I refrained from sighing deeply and loudly, while in my mind, I shook my head. "Problem?" I asked, taking a sip of wine.

He chuckled, uncomfortable as fuck. "I wouldn't call it a problem." He responded. "More like a, here we go with the typical independent woman stuff."

Ah man. *Wrong answer, Booboo.*

Calmly, I put my wine glass down on the table and collected my clutch and car keys that were on the chair next to me. "What are you doing?" He asked out of confusion.

"You're cute," I told him. "You're cute, you dress well, you have a great job where you make great money, and you sure know how to pick a good restaurant. But sadly, you're also painfully insecure about where you stand in this world as a man. Women who are sure of themselves and where they stand in this world, clearly make you highly uncomfortable. See, all I said was that I don't need a man to validate my existence. And all that means is that I am me—an individual with my own mind, thoughts, opinions, ambitions, beliefs, goals, qualities, and desires before a man comes into my life. And I will remain me—an individual with all of those same things, with a man in my life."

I pulled a crisp, twenty-dollar bill from my clutch, and placed it on the table as I stood. "I'm sure this will cover my glass of Pinot. Enjoy the rest of your evening, and take care of yourself. I meant that."

<u>Live *Your* Life.</u>

If you're single for too long, they'll tell you that you need to get out there, meet new people and date.

If you date more than two guys in a year though, they'll tell you that you need to slow down and learn how to be alone.

If you've spent a good chunk of your life lost, and kind of just winging it, they'll tell you to get your shit together.

But get your shit together now, and they'll whisper, negative, imaginary tales of what and who you did to come up.

If you're insecure, and have a hard time speaking up for yourself, they'll scream at you to get a backbone and be more confident.

Finally get that backbone, and some confidence, and they'll be sure to tell you that you think you're better than everyone.

Moral of the story is this:

People. Are. Batshit. Fucking. Nuts. Okay?

And you'd do good to practice ignoring the entire fuck outta them, so that you can live your damn life the way you want to and keep your sanity.

No, seriously.

Bossing Up.

I've learned through my own shit, that when you're genuinely ready to be the woman you want to be for yourself, you'll drop all of the excuses you once had, and you'll start making the moves that you need to make to become her.

Justified.

I don't cut people out of my life
randomly, because I'm "rude", "mean",
or "erratic".

I cut people out of my life consciously,
once it hits me that they aren't around
to add to my happiness, but rather take
from it.

Thoroughbred.

One thing people ask me all the time is, "After everything you've been through, how do you keep going?" My answer to that is this:

Every time things in my life get too heavy all at once, and I feel like I can't take it anymore, whenever it feels like I'm hanging onto my heart, soul and sanity by a single fucking thread—I stop and imagine what my life would be like twenty years from now if I were to give up on myself.

I imagine being fifty-two years old, looking at younger, hella successful authors and thinking to myself, *"I wonder if that could have been me had I just kept pushing."* I imagine being fifty-two years old looking at couples happily in love and thinking to myself, *"I wonder if that could have been me, had I just kept believing in love, instead of letting myself become and stay bitter."*

I imagine being fifty-two years old, broke, alone, living in a one-bedroom shithole apartment God knows where, miserable and bitter, waiting on a welfare check so I can do my groceries.

And that shit scares the *entire fuck* out of me.

All of that shit right there is all it takes for me to go back to the drawing board, and figure out how I'm going to push through whatever obstacles are in my way.

You see, I'm okay with failing a thousand times. Failing is how you learn to do and be better.

But I'm not okay with *being* a failure. Feel me?

There's a difference.

Life has knocked me down a million times without any apologies. Life has thrown me some painfully hard curve balls, watched me overcome them, decided it was going to throw some even harder curve balls, then sat there and watched if I would overcome those too. And it still does.

But I'm cool with it now, because I've matured enough to understand it.

How would I ever know what true happiness was, if I had never experienced true sadness? How would I ever know how to appreciate the good times I have, if I never experienced bad ones? How would I ever be able to fully understand the power of strength and resilience, if I'd never experienced the rock bottom feelings of weakness?

I don't think life is meant to be one steady stream of emotions or stability. I think it's meant to constantly push us in and out of our comfort zones in order to remind us of how we need to keep our faith, how important it is to trust ourselves, and to keep us learning and growing.

Be your own Boss.

Love yourself Fiercely.

Believe in yourself Immensely.

Invest in yourself Proudly.

Rinse and repeat, Forever.

We all need help in life sometimes, and that's normal.

A shoulder to lean on.

A loan when we're in a tight spot.

An ear to listen to us vent our frustrations.

A hand to hold.

A hug and a voice to whisper, *"Everything is gonna be alright. You'll see."*

But it's important to remember that no one can actually fix your life for you when it's broken. *You* have to fix your life when it's broken.

No one can remove you from your shitty ass relationship—you have to remove yourself.

No one can quit your shitty ass job that you hate so much—you have to quit it yourself.

No one can follow your dreams for you—you have to get off your ass and chase them yourself.

No one can stop the obstacles that life will put in your path to test you—you have to be the one to take a deep breath, get some courage and faith of *your own*, and jump, climb, crawl, and run through them yourself.

At the end of the day, other people can only help you so much. It's *your life*, and the fact is, you are one hundred percent <u>*responsible for yourself.*</u>

So to all of the girls out there with big dreams, in case no one told you, today—*you got this.*

Keep working hard and continue to stay focused on what you've got to do for YOU.

You're going to lose your balance and fall a million times. That's okay.

Get back up.

You're going to make a million mistakes. That's okay.

Learn from them.

You're going to have days when you feel like the entire world has ganged up to work against you, like shit couldn't possibly get any worse.

That's okay too.

It's all part of the process.
Trust me.

I know sometimes it feels like what you're working so hard to accomplish is taking forever. It's easy to want to just throw in the towel some days.

But please don't.

You owe it to yourself to one day sit in a reality that was once your dream, and be proud of yourself for making it all happen.

So again,
if no one told you today,
I will.

You got this.

Much Love.

Your Girl,

$\mathcal{B}$

GIRL POWER

GIRL

POWER

THE CRIMSON KISS QUOTE COLLECTION

II

INSTAGRAM-FACEBOOK-TWITTER@THECRIMSONKISS

Previous books by Cici.B

Letters to My Ex

Blush

Lost and Found: The Book of Short Stories

Spilled Words: The Crimson Kiss Quote Collection

12:02AM Volume I: Exploring B

Printed in Great Britain
by Amazon

58671612R00092